AF609175

NOTHING MINOR

nothing Minor

a 2019 summer journey covering minor league baseball

ANDREW SNORTON

EmoryRose Photography

Creative Community Solutions, LLC

First Printing, 2020

Photography: Andrew Snorton and EmoryRose Photography

Website: Andrew Snorton via Wix.com

For book signings, readings, and speaking engagements, please send all inquiries to authorasnorton@gmail.com or asnorton-ccs@gmail.com.

www.asnortonccs.com or asnortonccs.wixsite.com/authorpage

Social media: Author Andrew Snorton (Facebook), @authorasnorton (Instagram and Twitter), and Author ASnorton (YouTube).

ISBN: 978-0-578-72358-7
ISBN (E-version): 978-0-578-72359-4

Dedication

This is respectfully dedicated to my Dad
with whom
I learned to truly enjoy the game and
comradery
that comes with it.

To Jackie Robinson, Larry Doby, and
others
who changed the game.

To the players who are in relentless
pursuit of their passion
to work their way up from the
minor leagues to Major League Baseball.

And that's ***nothing Minor.***

Contents

Introduction

Welcome to nothing Minor

Before being the "national pastime", the grand old game, a game of hardball, or on the diamond, baseball is simply the game I watch and enjoy time to bond with my Dad.

I recall many a Saturday afternoon anticipating the Major League Baseball Game of the Week (along with a few games I'd watch at night, especially sneaking a peek on a "school-night" after I'm supposed to be asleep), sitting on the couch with a slice of pizza and some Kool Aid while he'd have pizza and a grown man's beverage. Our discussions would include the subject of math in the form of batting averages (the number of hits divided by the number of official plate appearances), pitch counts, and other statistics. It's more like an athletic version of playing chess as you are constantly processing all of this information, juxtaposed with the game situations, shifts, someone's tendencies, and other variables well before the pitch is released; all this is done while the batter is looking at arm angles and the pitcher's deliveries, simply to hit a baseball coming at you 90 miles per hour or more from a mere ***60 feet and 6 inches away.***

However, it's more than just crunching numbers and compiling data; there's history lessons as well. Pioneers like Jackie Robinson, Larry Doby, Roy Campanella, Satchel Paige, and yes, the traditional greats like Babe Ruth, Joe DiMaggio, and others are part of the history, both living and recorded. Even in elementary school, seeing my favorite team, the New York Yankees, and watching future Hall of Fame players such as (but not limited to) Reggie Jackson, Rod Carew, Steve Carlton, and Robin Yount, to others who aren't in Cooperstown but made their mark like Willie Randolph, Roy White, and yes, even that team in Queens, from area favorites including Hubie Brooks and Mookie Wilson, are among the players who draw me to the game. The classic ***"Reggie, REGGIE"*** chants in the 1977 World Series (and the Game 6 clincher against the Los Angeles Dodgers when he hits 3 consecutive home runs on 3 swings) are just some of the epic memories I have of the game of baseball.

Still, there's another part of the game that sometimes gets overlooked, and in reality, is a true "hidden jewel"; that is where many a player gets their professional start, Minor League Baseball. Most players earn their keep at Rookie League, A Ball, AA Ball, and AAA Ball (which is a level below the Major Leagues). And this is where legends are truly made.

From small towns to mid-sized cities (and even some larger metropolitan areas), these spaces and places have a "Field of Dreams" feel to it, as most players who make it to "the show" (there are a few exceptions such as players like Bob Horner and Barry Bonds who make the jump from college baseball to the Atlanta Braves and Pittsburgh Pirates respectively, along with players who play overseas like Ichiro Suzuki) get their start here. Recent Hall of Famer (and current part of the Miami Marlins' ownership team) Derek Jeter, along with former NL Most Valuable Player Christian Yelich (of the Milwaukee Brewers), and the New York Yankees' Giancarlo Stanton are among those who have Greensboro, NC as one of their minor league baseball stops. Now with the Los Angeles Dodgers, former American League MVP Mookie Betts has Greenville, SC as one of his stops on his major league baseball journey, and players including Freddie Freeman and Ronald Acuña of the Atlanta Braves (Gwinnett County, GA), the Minnesota Twins' Jose Berrios (Chattanooga, TN), the White Sox' future infielder/outfielder Nick Madigral (Birmingham, AL), and Hall of Famer Chipper Jones (Pearl, MS) are among those whose travels to the big leagues include stops on the minor league circuit.

The on-field photography, pre/post-game interviews, and game coverage make ***June-August 2019*** a memorable time for me and others able to witness some amazing on field play. Covering 7 games in 8 weeks is considerable movement in and of itself, and when you include coverage around the Major League Baseball Trade Deadline (July 31st), some of the moves include players that I covered inching closer to their Major League goals, including a few who are promoted to big league rosters. This edition takes a look at the Gwinnett Stripers (AAA affiliate of the Atlanta Braves), the Chattanooga Lookouts (AA affiliate of the Cincinnati Reds), Greenville Drive (A affiliate of the Boston Red Sox), Greensboro Grasshoppers (A affiliate of the Pittsburgh Pirates), Birmingham Barons (AA affiliate of the Chicago White Sox), and Mississippi Braves (AA affiliate of the Atlanta Braves). Enjoy the views along with the larger stories of dreaming and working towards your goals, and staying connected with the game.

And that is nothing minor.

A game winning scene for the Mississippi Braves (Trustmark Park in Pearl, MS).
Andrew Snorton

Views from Cool-Ray Field, Fleur Field (upper left and right), Regions Field, and Trustman Park (lower left and right)
Andrew Snorton

Chapter 1

It's Greater in Gwinnett

June 18, 2019. About 5pm, making my way through a light rain, I finally pull into Cool-Ray Field in Lawrenceville, GA.

It is the home of the Gwinnett Stripers, the AAA affiliate of the Atlanta Braves, just one level below the Major Leagues. Formerly located in Richmond, VA (as the Richmond Braves), their move to Metro-Atlanta starts with keeping the name of their parent team before their transition to their current name. Regardless of the name, the story of players at this level is making the final jump to getting their proverbial "cup of coffee".

A few players are part of the Atlanta Braves' 40-man roster; during the regular season, a team would carry 25 players (until the September 1st expanded roster callups), but their 40-man roster means some players at the AAA level (and in a few cases, the AA roster) are part of the big league team's active roster; they are literally one phone call or personnel move away from being in the big leagues.

After checking in, I start my coverage with a pre-game interview with a player who is ***this close*** to the Major Leagues, Travis Demeritte. The 2018 AA (Mississippi Braves) Player of the Year (for the Braves' system), a New York City born/Winder (GA) raised player is originally a 1st round draft pick of the Texas Rangers in the 2013 Major League Baseball draft; he's part of a trade-deadline deal from the Texas system to the Atlanta system in 2016 as an infielder (shortstop), but later is shifted to the outfield. As a top-20 prospect within the Braves' system, at the time of the game, his 17 homeruns and 63 runs batted in rank him in the top-10 in both key categories for the International League.

"I think that if you want to go far in this game (obviously), guys at the highest level are very consistent on a daily basis; just having a routine I can fall back on when things are going good or going bad is big for me", he notes in our interview. Paying attention to his offensive approach, including continuing to work on his defense (again, he previously is a shortstop and is currently playing right-field), are keys for his progress as a player.

But it's more than an individual game. The team's comradery is important; the blend of veteran and younger players (including those on the AAA/MLB "shuttle") is central to the team's success, including learning and knowing how to win games and executing on as high a level as possible.

Their game against the Louisville Bats (the AAA affiliate of the Cincinnati Reds) gets underway after a rain delay lasting nearly 2 hours (pushing the first pitch closer to 9pm EST). Gwinnett starter Kolby Allard, a top-10 prospect within the

Braves' system (and their 1st round pick in the 2015 draft) takes the "hill" for the team. He enters the game with a 1-0 record in his 2 previous starts (15 innings pitched, allowing only 2 runs in those starts, with 12 strikeouts and 3 walks).

Early in the game, a runner's interference call against Adam Duvall (who in 2016 makes the Major League Baseball All-Star team as a member of the Cincinnati Reds) and Stripers' manager (and former MLB catcher) Damon Berryhill ejection gets the team off to a rocky start. However, by the time they enter the top of the 6th inning, they have a 2-0 lead. With key hits (and runs batted in/RBI's) by outfielder Rafael Ortega (who would get 2 hits in 4 at-bats) and second baseman Jack Lopez (who goes 4 for 4), it seems like the team is on their way to another victory.

However, Louisville explodes for 3 runs in the top of the 6th inning. Allard still has a solid game (6 innings pitched with 9 strikeouts and 3 walks), but down 3-2 and approaching a late game situation is something the team is challenged to overcome in getting back in the game.

Pre-game with Travis Demeritte.
Andrew Snorton

With a renewed focus, they do just that.

Down by a run in the bottom of the 9th inning, the Stripers rally thanks to singles by Lopes and Demeritte; a hit-by-pitch by Andres Blanco loads the bases with one out. Once first baseman Sean Kazmar, Jr comes to the plate, he unleashes a rocket off the delivery by the Bats' closer, Sal Romano. A great catch and play by centerfielder Narcisco Crook leads to Demeritte getting thrown out at 3rd base to end the inning, but not before Lopes scores to tie the game.

And this leads to extra innings, along with an opportunity to complete the comeback and get a win.

Duvall, who is part of the Braves' 40-man roster (and is among the AAA/International League leaders in homeruns and RBI's), showcases the team's resiliency and winning ways. His 2-run blast off the Bats' Romano ends the game as the team earns a 5-3 extra innings win (10 innings).

Kolby Allard of the Gwinnett Stripers.
A top prospect, his 6-inning effort
keeps the team in the game.
Andrew Snorton

A game seemingly under control, a run by the visiting team, and then seeing the home team pull out a victory is a thrilling experience. Even with the "game within the game", the themes of focus, hard-work, dedication, and teamwork are among the attributes the Stripers display in their victory. Not only are they focused on their individual goals, but together, everyone achieves more, a true measure of a team.

"Don't give up; silence the noise. Continue; if it's your dream and that's what you want to do, don't let anyone deter you from it, and stay resilient", Demeritte notes during our interview before the game; with the win in hand, those words ring even louder given the game outcome.

Resiliency. There's ***nothing*** minor about that.

Travis Demeritte's (top-10 in AAA in homeruns and RBI's at the time of the game) helps the Stripers stay at the top of the standings.
Andrew Snorton

Adam Duvall at the plate. A member of the 40-man roster, he's a leading presence on the team.
Andrew Snorton

A winning view from the press box.
Andrew Snorton

Chapter 2

Be on the Lookout

When good friends get together, you may want to be on the lookout. Their chemistry can lead to a positive thing, including a blend of the serious, sincere, and downright silly.

Both hailing from Metro-Atlanta, Taylor Trammell and Tyler Stephenson epitomize this creative balance. From their friendship to competing with and against each other, to talking with them on a late June afternoon (June 29, 2019) before their game against the Tennessee Smokies (the AA affiliate of the Chicago Cubs), the outfielder and catcher play key roles for the Chattanooga Lookouts (the AA affiliate of the Cincinnati Reds). Their energy and passion for the game are indicative of being ranked as the #1 and #5 prospects in the entire Reds' organization.

Trammell notes the importance of taking no days off.

He comments, "Every day, you're working on something new. You're continuously growing and getting in a consistent mindset. Since I was drafted (in 2016 out of high school), that's played a huge role in my career".

His teammate and friend (Stephenson) builds upon this philosophy as he notes, “Figuring out a routine that you can do consistently to prepare yourself (is big); health is important as last year was my first full healthy season (and) we want to win a ring (Southern League Championship)”.

As for the actual game (which is a promotional night, “Superhero Night”), the Lookouts jump out to an early 3-0 lead thanks to a RBI single by starting pitcher Scott Moss (who not only goes 1 for 2, but pitches 5 innings, allowing 2 runs on 6 hits, and striking out 8 batters and walking 2 batters).

In the top of the 5th inning, the Smokies strike back thanks to shortstop Zach Short (who goes 2 for 5 with a RBI) and catcher PJ Higgins (who goes 2 for 4 with 2 RBI’s), making it a 3-2 game. Chattanooga would respond in the bottom of the inning thanks to a 3-RBI double by right-fielder Ibandel Isabel to

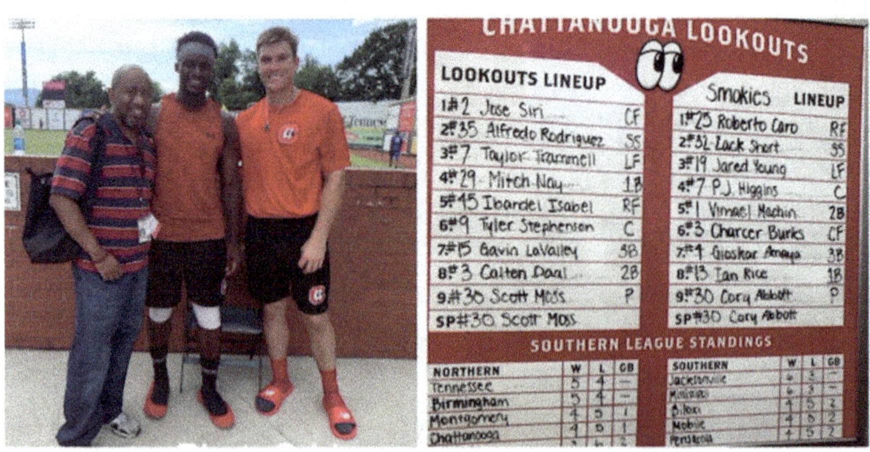

Pre-game with Travis Trammell (center) and Tyler Stephenson (right) as well as a look at the lineups. Both are top-5 prospects (#1 and #5 respectively) in the Reds' system and are lifelong friends.

EmoryRose Photography

A "mashup" of the game action between the Tennessee Smokies and Chattanooga Lookouts, including some "superhero" action.
Andrew Snorton

make it a 6-2 game, and by the time first-baseman Mitch Nay launches a solo home-run in the bottom of the 7th (he would go 4 for 5 with 2 RBI's), the Lookouts are up 7-2 and would eventually earn an 8-4 win.

After the win, there's not much time to celebrate the series-ending game.

Once the fireworks end, they are on their charter bus to Jacksonville to start a series. On Sunday. Yes, the ***very next day.***

A look from the press box.
Andrew Snorton

It's part of the process.

As Tyler and Travis note, it's about a routine and being as consistent as possible to achieve their individual and team goals.

However, July 31, 2019 changes the teammate situation, but certainly not the friendship.

Trammell is part of a 3-team trade deadline deal between the Reds, Cleveland Indians, and San Diego Padres. Trevor Bauer (starting pitcher) is traded from Cleveland to Cincinnati; Yasiel Puig (outfielder from Cincinnati), Scott Moss (pitcher from Cincinnati), Franmil Reyes (outfielder from San Diego), along with prospects Logan Allen (pitcher) and infielder Victor Nova (both from San Diego's system) are traded to Cleveland.

Trammell ends up with San Diego, as they envision him being a top-of-the order player batting ahead of rising star Fernando Tatis, Jr (their starting shortstop) and big free agent (2019) signee, Manny Machado (third-baseman).

The game, focus, and moves made clearly are nothing minor.

Game action
Andrew Snorton

A game action montage.
EmoryRose Photography

Twilight in Chattanooga.
Andrew Snorton

Reading and reviewing game notes, and catching the pre-game view.
Andrew Snorton

Chapter 3

Driving the Palmetto State Rivalry

July 6, 2019 is another edition of the rivalry between the Boston Red Sox and New York Yankees. Well, it's on the A level, and while not exactly the same as arguably Major League Baseball's greatest rivalry, the Palmetto State version between the Greenville Drive (the Boston Red Sox A ball affiliate) and Charleston River Dogs (the New York Yankees A ball affiliate) has its own character and energy.

This is an epic and rare 5-game series that takes place prior to the All-Star Weekend on the Major and Minor League level. With players on this level, the focus goes beyond honing their skills in ascending and pursuing their dreams of being on a big-league roster. Flour Field is essentially the minor league version of Fenway Park, as they have their own "Green Monster" in left field so their players can replicate the nuisances of their big-league brethren.

Prior to their game, infielder Brandon Howlett takes time to share with me his early lessons on this level and how they can parlay to success on larger levels. A year removed from high school (and the Red Sox' #15 rated prospect in their entire system), the 19-year old shares with me some of the things already learned and how to apply them to help with his maturation in the game.

"You always work. You always grind. I make sure I don't get too high or too low. Staying even-keeled is important", he notes.

Even as a 19-year old, his insight speaks volumes.

And onto the game in a rivalry like none other. Even on a mid-summer day in Greenville, the intensity that you'd anticipate at Fenway Park or Yankee Stadium, let alone both larger cities, is felt here.

Let's get to it, shall we?

The Drive strikes first in the Palmetto State Rivalry; in the bottom of the first inning, thanks to singles by right-fielder Tyler Esplin and Triston Casas (getting runners on 1st and 3rd base and pictured below), Devlin Granberg's (first-baseman) single puts the team up 1-0. The River Dogs return the favor in the top of the 3rd inning as Canaan Smith (left-fielder) hits a double to drive in a run to tie the game. In the top of the 4th inning, Charleston catcher Eduardo Navas notches an RBI double to make it a 2-1 game.

Greenville at the plate.
Andrew Snorton

Before the game, Brandon Howell, a top-15 prospect in the Boston (Red Sox) system, takes time to sit down with us.
Andrew Snorton

Game action between the Greenville Drive (A affiliate of the Boston Red Sox) and the Charleston River Dogs (A affiliate of the New York Yankees).
Andrew Snorton

Then comes the top of the 5th inning, and for a moment, the River Dogs look a little like their Bronx Bombers namesakes.

Shortstop Max Burt cranks out a 3-run homerun to chase Greenville starter Chris Machamer (he lasts 4.1 innings but allows 5 earned runs and allows 5 walks) to put Charleston ahead 5-1. They add to their lead in the top of the 6th inning thanks to designated hitter Eric Wagman's RBI single and a sacrifice fly (RBI) by first-baseman Mickey Gasper to put the lead at 7-1.

Although Greenville makes a valiant effort, the relief pitching of the River Dogs keeps the Drive in "park"; their relievers allow 2 hits in 4.1 innings pitched, and reliever Tanner Myatt (2.1 innings pitched) gets the win.

Despite the loss to their rivals, the team's professionalism shines through in my post-game interview with Tristan Casas (who goes 1 for 4). It can be a challenge to interview a player after a loss as you really can't anticipate (even with a cooling off period) how they'll respond. However, taken 26th overall in the 2018 Major League Baseball Draft (and turning down an offer to play college baseball at the University of Miami), the #2 rated prospect in the Red Sox system speaks with a level of maturity typically associated with veteran players at the MLB level.

He notes, "We stayed in it and battled to the last out. I think we learned a lot (about our team) and can take that with us to the next game". In assessing Charleston, he adds, "They have a lot of hard throwers. We have to look to be aggressive early in the zone; we know we're going to be challenged, so we have to come out with the right approach".

That statement provides some understanding that even at this level (A Ball), the importance of reviewing scouting reports and other details is critical for success at this (or any) level.

And when it comes to losing, he concludes, "We either learn, or we win".

Greenville trying to get back in the game against Charleston.
Andrew Snorton

A view from the Drive dugout.
Andrew Snorton

The camera crew catching the game action.
Andrew Snorton

A quick game break.
Andrew Snorton

Vantage points from the camera pits and press box.
Andrew Snorton

We either learn, or we win (Tristian Casas).
Andrew Snorton

Night falls.
Andrew Snorton

Chapter 4

Galavanting with the Grasshoppers

Ah, the Triad.

This is a favorite space and place for me, the region of the Tarheel State (North Carolina) where Winston-Salem, High Point, and Greensboro come together. About a 30-minute drive from my alma mater (Wake Forest University) is the 'Boro. Yes, it's about those long-ago and recent visits on both ends of Market Street (UNC-Greensboro to the west and NC A&T to the east), a stop by Dame's Chicken and Waffles, and taking in history at the International Civil Rights Center and Museum (formerly the Woolworth's Building where the first sit-ins take place). And while Winston-Salem and High Point have their teams (the Winston-Salem Dash, an A affiliate of the Chicago White Sox, along with the High Point Rockers, an independent baseball league team), my first dose of minor league baseball (as a college student) is in Greensboro.

This is when they used to be known as the Greensboro Hornets and played in the old War Memorial Stadium. And ironically, a high school classmate of mine by the name of Tim Flannelly played third-base for the team (he would get a cup of coffee with the New York Yankees), along with me winning a crowd giveaway of a free Domino's Pizza during one of the game breaks. You were supposed to win it by making the most noise, but I made eye contact with the young lady who was doing the giveaway, and the rest is history (meaning me and my high school and college classmate Ryan Bifulco ate well that game).

But I digress.

In the same city where recent major league names including Hall of Fame shortstop Derek Jeter, Don Mattingly, Christian Yelich, and Giancarlo Stanton, along with historic figures such as Satchel Paige and Johnny Mize made their way through the ranks, the same is taking place today with the Greensboro Grasshoppers, the A affiliate of the Pittsburgh Pirates. On a warm summer evening (July 13, 2019), I get to experience the game from First National Bank Field.

Nestled in downtown Greensboro, the ballpark is a symbol of the growth and rebirth of different parts of the city. And the same holds true for the team, as their 56-34 overall record (at the time of the game) has them in the playoff hunt.

Prior to the game against the West Virginia Power (the A ball affiliate of the Seattle Mariners), right-fielder Josh Davis takes time to speak with me, by far the longest pre-game interview I've done to this point, but it really is (as are all of the other interviews) extremely engaging and eye-opening. If not for the game, we likely would have carried on with our conversation even longer, as the University of California product shows a deep understanding of his individual and team's growth, especially in the heat of a playoff race.

"Being consistent, keeping the same swing, and not trying to do too much at the plate (are the things I'm focused on", he shares as his recent hot streak is a by-product of this strategic approach. "I'm seeing the ball a lot better and swinging the bat better; my goal is to keep that same consistency throughout the season".

In his first full season of professional baseball, he emphasizes the importance of having fun and enjoying the game. Given the length of the season and the highs and lows that come with it, loving the game, having friends on the team, remaining confident, and having a positive mindset are essential in order to be successful at this (or any level).

A view from the press box of the field and emerging skyline of Greensboro, NC
Andrew Snorton

And even with failure, there's ***perspective.***

He adds, "You're not going to get a hit (or homerun) every time or (as a pitcher) strike every batter out. You're going to go on cold streaks, but the main thing is to stay positive and know that hit or strikeout is going to come. Once you feel it one time, your confidence comes back and the next thing you know, you're going to play the way you want to play".

Veteran insight from younger players is clearly a sign of understanding and a level of maturity that positions them to be successful. And when it comes to the actual game, the topics Davis talks about comes to light.

Trailing 1-0 in the bottom of the 2nd inning, Greensboro's offense gets in gear. A double by third-baseman Michael Gretler is followed by a defensive miscue by West Virginia third-baseman Bobby Honeyman off the bat of designated hitter Zack Kone, making it a tie game (1-1). The following batter, catcher Zac Susi, is hit by a pitch from Power starter Steven Moyers; back-to-back RBI singles by top prospects second-baseman Ji-Hwan Bae (who goes 3 for 4 with 1 RBI) and center-fielder Fabricio Macias (3 for 5 with 1 RBI) put the Grasshoppers ahead 3-1.

And speaking of Davis, he gets one of the kinds of hits he refers to in our interview. In the bottom of the 3rd inning, his monster solo shot makes it a 4-1 lead for Greensboro. Although West Virginia's Joseph Rosa (who goes 3 for 4 with a run batted in) makes it a 4-2 game in the top of the 4th, it appears the Grasshoppers are in control of the game.

Then, things change rather quickly.

In the top of the 5th inning, West Virginia chases Greensboro starter Steven Jennings (4.2 innings pitched, allowing 5 runs) as they erupt for 6 runs. Paced by first-baseman Onil Pena's 3-run bomb (homerun), their 6-run inning puts the Power ahead 8-4. The Grasshoppers "hop" back into it in the bottom half of the inning, as Davis' leadoff bunt (he goes 3 for 5 in the game with a homerun and 2 RBI's) leads to a 2- run inning to get the team within striking distance (8-6) and subsequently knocking out Power starter Steven Moyers (5 innings pitched, 6 runs allowed/3 earned) from the game. By the top of the 7th inning, Greensboro ties the game (8-8), but West Virginia responds with 2-run inning to take a 10-8 lead and hang on for the win. Not the desired outcome, but their ability to compete is what keeps them in the mix; that is nothing minor.

Pre-game along with in-game with Josh Davis.
Andrew Snorton

Both teams dig in during the back and forth affair.
Andrew Snorton

In game action with Greensboro's Zac Susi catching.
Andrew Snorton

Carolina, the Triad, and twilight on my mind.
Andrew Snorton

A back and forth game between both teams; you can sense the intensity from the dugout.
Andrew Snorton

Chapter 5

Bold Play by the Barons

Back in 1994, a former basketball player by the name of Michael Jordan "rode the bus" to Birmingham. In his lone year playing for the Birmingham Barons, the AA affiliate of the Chicago White Sox, his .202 average might not have been the greatest. However, considering he had not played in more than 10 years (since high school), in 127 games, he drove in 51 runs and stole 30 bases.

Fast forward to July 21, 2019 on a slightly overcast day, the Barons enter their game at Regions Field a ½ game out of first place (2nd half of the season), showing vast improvement compared to the first half of the season (27-42, 16.5 games out of 1st place).

With highly regarded organizational prospects including outfielder Luis Basabe (#7 prospect), outfield Luis Gonzalez (#10 prospect), 2018 1st round pick Nick Madrigal (infielder), infielder Laz Rivera (#17 prospect), fellow Wake Forest alum Gavin Sheets (#18 prospect), and former 1st round pick (2014 of the Milwaukee Brewers) Kodi Medeiros (a pitcher who is on the White Sox' 40 man active roster), the team is starting to realize its potential. Add the leadership of manager and arguably one of the top shortstops in his 24-year Major League Career, Omar Vizquel, along with MLB veterans Charlie Poe, Richard Dotson, and Wes Helms (the coaching staff), the team has capable personnel at the helm guiding them during their second half push.

Third-baseman Ti'Quan Forbes takes time with me pre-game to share his perspective on the season, including their second half improvement. A former 2nd round pick of the Texas Rangers (2014), he is putting things together in his 2nd full season in the White Sox system.

"It's getting late in the season; (I just) keep on working, playing hard, and having fun with my teammates", he opens.

With a 5-for-11 performance in their current series against the Tennessee Smokies (who are the AA affiliate of the Chicago Cubs, their big-league cross-town rivals in the Windy

Ti'Quan Forbes brings a positive energy and insight during our pre-game interview and the game at large.
Andrew Snorton

City), his focus is on individual and team improvement. Even with the possible distractions of post-season play, the trade deadline (July 31st), and late season callups (to AAA or even the 40-man roster starting September 1st), he is staying locked in on the here and now.

"You take it one step at a time; if it (a callup or trade) happens, it happens. You still have to keep it together; you are playing for more than just getting called up", he advises.

With a presence and energy that is borderline contagious, team morale is key. He notes, "Handshakes. Dancing. We have a game we play (Pop and Cup), and we just talk with each other. We keep that energy up for each other".

And he has some advice for players of all levels when it comes to the game.

"If you're going to do this, you have to do it for the long haul. Baseball's tough; keep grinding and take it one day at a time. You're going to fail more than not; a .300 hitter (getting hits in 30% of your at-bats) is good in baseball. Continue to work; go after it. If you dream about it chase your dream", he emphasizes.

The energy from the interview surfaces in the actual game. Well, not initially.

After spotting the Barons a 1-0 lead, the Smokies tag the Barons with a 6-run 4th inning as Birmingham starter Tanner Banks (3.1 innings pitched, allowing 6 runs) is knocked out of the game. Outfielder Charcer Burks gets the scoring started with a RBI double (tying the game at 1). Infielder/Outfielder Christian Donahue's ground-rule double scores 2 runners, making it a 3-1 game. A single by outfielder Roberto Caro (2 RBI's) and a sacrifice fly by shortstop Nico Hoerner makes it a 6-1 game.

In the bottom of the 4th, the team's 2nd half of the season resiliency comes to light. Thanks to a solo homerun by third-baseman Damek Tomscha (who goes 4 for 5 with 4 RBI's) and a surprising 2-run homerun by catcher Alfredo Gonzalez (his first of the season), the Barons get back in the game, trailing by a 6-4 margin. They keep the momentum going in the bottom the 5th inning. With outfielder Blake Rutherford scoring on a wild pitch and another RBI by Tomscha, the game is tied at 6.

An outstanding pitching effort by the Barons' bullpen (5.2 innings pitched, allowing zero runs) keeps the team in position

One of the top prospects for the White Sox, Luis Gonzalez, at the plate.
Andrew Snorton

to complete the comeback. Once the bottom of the 9th inning arrives, the team takes it up a notch.

Sounds moves by Vizquel sets the stage, as Sheets leads the inning off with a double. Forbes takes one for the team, as he is hit by a pitch. With runners on 1st and 2nd base, the hot-hitting Tomscha deposits a single to left field, leading to the team's come-from-behind win (7-6).

In the post-game interview, Tomscha, the player of the game, echoes the key ideas shared in Forbes' pre-game interview. He shares his work ethic for the game by stating, "I got here pretty early to work on a few things with my swing, as well as getting comfortable with my swing; I feel like I did a pretty good job today staying with my approach".

And as for team? He reiterates, "This team has a bunch of high-energy guys; there's no quit in this team".

Bold individual and team play; that is ***nothing minor.***

The Windy City Rivalry on the AA level.
Andrew Snorton

From the field to the press box. And Forbes in the field (on base).
Andrew Snorton

The Barons in-between innings.
Andrew Snorton

Top prospect Nick Madrigal steps up to the plate.
Andrew Snorton

First-baseman (and Wake Forest alum)
Gavin Sheets at-bat.
Andrew Snorton

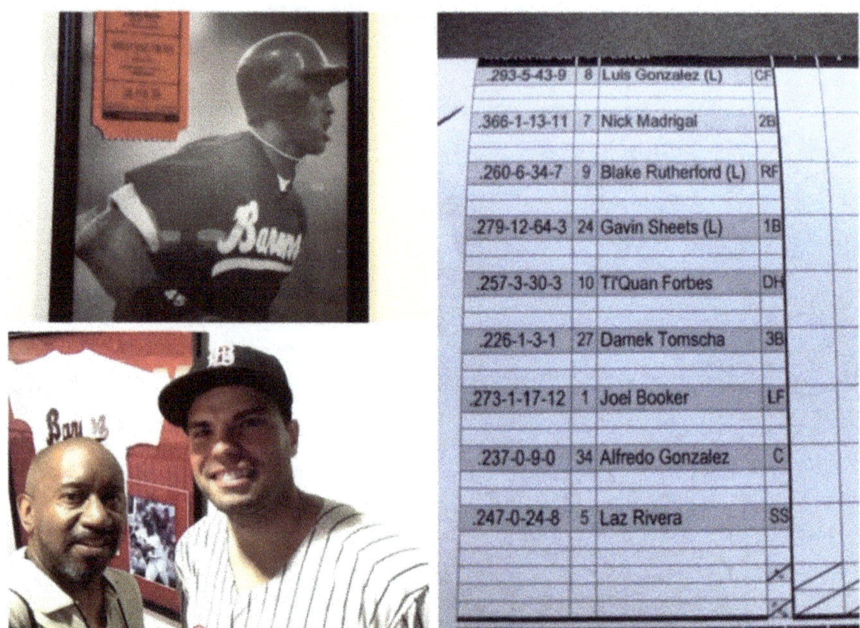

Snapshots of Michael Jordan (yes, he played here for a season), the lineups, and player of the game Damek Tomscha.
Andrew Snorton

Teamwork.
Andrew Snorton

Winners!
Andrew Snorton

A great view of the park and the city of Birmingham, AL.
Andrew Snorton

Chapter 6

Seeing trade-day changes in the Stripers

There and back again? Somewhat, but not exactly.

Our return to Coolray Field on July 31, 2019 brings about some changes. Many are aware this day is the trade deadline; while attention is typically given to player movement in MLB, people forget how active player movement is on this level.

Our pre-game interviewee from last time, Travis Demeritte, is traded to the Detroit Tigers (along with Joey Wentz) in the Shane Greene deal; Atlanta's need for relief pitching at the back end of their bullpen (closer) is the main reason for the trade, and while Demeritte (who is hitting .286 with 24 home runs and 74 RBI at the time of the trade) is initially moved to the Toledo Mud Hens (the Tigers' AAA team), the big league club purchases his contract. As a result, he closes out the season (August-October) as the team's primary right-fielder.

Kolby Allard gets traded to the Texas Rangers for relief pitcher Chris Martin. After a start with the Nashville Sounds (the Rangers' AAA team), he gets promoted to the Texas Rangers (and goes 4-2 with a 4.96 ERA), positioning himself for a spot in the team's starting rotation for 2020. And Adam Duvall, due to an injury to the Braves' starting right fielder, Nick Markakis, is recalled to serve as the primary right-fielder down the stretch as the team makes the playoffs (but loses to the St Louis Cardinals in the National League Division Series 3 games to 2).

One player who can relate to being on the MLB/Minor League "shuttle" is pitcher Touki Toussaint. After a call-up in 2018, he is on the team's 40-man roster, spending time with both the Braves and the Stripers. Before the game between the Norfolk Tides (41-67), Toussaint shares his experience, along with the team's overall focus as they are in 1st place (64-44 and leading their division) in pursuit of a playoff spot.

The proverbial "working on his game" emanates throughout our interview.

"My fastball command (is key); just being able to slow the game down (is helping me improve). My delivery (is something else I'm working on); if I'm struggling, I know what I can go back to", he shares. While he has a 4-0 record in his big-league stint (along with 45 strikeouts in 41.2 innings pitched), his command is something to continue to work on (as he has a 5.62 ERA). However, his youth (23), along with his work ethic, are bound to have him back with the Braves, especially with realizing and improving his performance and overall consistency.

He stresses, "You have to be consistent; consistency is key. If you are a bullpen guy, for 8 out of 10 games, you better be on your "A-game"; if you're a starter, and if you have 35 starts (considered the average or target number if a team has a 5-man starting rotation), you need to have (at least) 25 to 30 good starts and maybe 5 all-right ones".

Clearly, he has a growing command of his performance and mindset needed to get recalled and remain in the Major Leagues.

The same goes for the rest of the team.

Pre-game with Touki Touissant (upper left), working the camera pits (upper right), Jack Lopez in the batter's box (lower left), and Andres Blanco (lower right).
Andrew Snorton and EmoryRose Photography

Kyle Wright draws the start for Gwinnett. His dominant performance (7 innings pitched, allowing 1 run on 4 hits, along with 8 strikeouts) keeps Norfolk at bay. Thanks to a 4th inning solo home run by catcher Alex Jackson and a 5th inning 3-run home run by second baseman Andres Blanco, the Stripers put 4 runs on the board to pull away from the Tides.

Although Norfolk outfielder Mason Williams gets a run-scoring single in the top of the 6th inning, it's a sound 4-1 win for Gwinnett as they make continue making their playoff push.

As player of the game Andres Blanco shares post-game, "I have improved this year. I want to do my best every single day; even if it goes wrong, it doesn't matter. Something good is going to happen".

Starting pitcher Kyle Wright (7 IP, 1 ER, and 8 strikeouts) and catcher Alex Jackson call a great game for the Stripers.
Andrew Snorton

Then he takes a moment to pause. Akin to the words of the late guitarist Jimi Hendrix, “Wisdom speaks”, he delivers a telling statement.

“It (my mindset) hasn’t always happened (in my 19-year baseball career), but now, I’m proud of myself and where I am (as his homerun set a career high, 15). I’m having a good time, having fun, and when put in a position to be a hero, here I am”.

Individual growth. Collective growth. Maturity, combined with a love and passion for the game, and pursuit of your professional dreams. Be it a younger or older player, while sometimes taking different paths, it’s about getting to the same destination, the Major Leagues.

Game action between Gwinnett and Norfolk.
Andrew Snorton and EmoryRose Photography

Those are just a few of the reasons minor league baseball is one of those hidden jewels, and in returning to where the coverage starts, it's a reminder of why I'm taking time to share these and other stories, especially on trade deadline day.

And that is ***nothing minor.***

Rafael Ortega (#5) greets Andres Blanco after he hits a homerun. The team is in the mix for a playoff spot and their overall play keeps them in 1st place.
Andrew Snorton

Post-game with player of the game Andres Blanco.
EmoryRose Photography

Chapter 7

Major moves in Mississippi

The 'Sip!

I mean Mississippi, specifically, Pearl (MS). Literally a stone's throw away from Jackson., it's not too far from the state capital, the home of the late Medgar Evers, and a favorite space in what I call the "rebirth" district, Johnny T's Bistro and Blues.

And it's the home of the Mississippi Braves, the AA affiliate of the Atlanta Braves.

A number of players make this one of their minor league stops. Players including (but not limited to) Ronald Acuña, Jr (Atlanta Braves), Travis Demeritte (Detroit Tigers), Mallex Smith (Atlanta Braves, Tampa Bay Rays, and Seattle Mariners), Ozzie Albies (Atlanta Braves), Tommy LaStella (Atlanta Braves, Chicago Cubs, and Anaheim Angels), Andrelton Simmons (Atlanta Braves and Anaheim Angels), Dansby Swanson (Atlanta Braves), Evan Gattis (Atlanta Braves and Houston Astros), Mike

Minor (Atlanta Braves and Texas Rangers), Julio Teheran (Atlanta Braves and Anaheim Angels), and Alex Wood (Atlanta Braves, Los Angeles Dodgers, and Cincinnati Reds) are among players over the past decade who have played here.

And then there's players including Trey Harris and 2019 1st round draft pick Braden Shewmake who are among those looking to follow the trend of making a major move in Mississippi.

Harris, a Metro-Atlanta native and University of Missouri alum, is a 2018 draft pick, taken in the 32nd round. Where you are drafted is nice, but what you do with the opportunity is nicer. And his efforts since being drafted have him locked in as a key player for the team and a player on the rise and on the Braves' radar. His approach, as is the case with other players, is more veteran-like. After sharing his work habits on his game, including his offense, he delivers this nugget in making success more reachable.

He advises, ""I look at my at-bats in tens (and try to go 3 for 10 every single time). In looking at the game in smaller increments, it allows me to compete at a high level".

In addition to reinforcing many of the concepts other players share about the importance of one's work ethic and habits, as well as building bonds with your teammates, he adds this for younger players of all levels.

"Play hard every day. If you don't leave the field dirty, you aren't successful. And people do pay attention (whether or not you play hard)".

Clearly, he gets the memo, and so does his teammate, Braden Shewmake.

One of the Braves' ***two 1st round picks of the 2019 MLB Draft (23rd overall),*** the former Texas A&M Aggie makes a fast rise through the ranks. After "raking" in Rome (the Braves' A affiliate), he is making his AA debut (in this game). What makes this impressive is ***he is the first*** of any of the members of his draft class to reach AA. And for additional personal intrigue, they are playing a team I covered previously, the Birmingham Barons.

The Braves' Nolan KIngham and the Barons' Blake Battenfield provide their teams with quality starts. The first hit of the game doesn't take place until the bottom of the 3rd inning by Mississippi's Riley Unroe. When the bottom of the 6th inning comes, it ironically ends up being Shewmake and Harris who make things happen.

Shewmake's (he goes 1 for 4) infield single gets him on base for Harris. A few pitches later, he deposits a 2-run rocket into

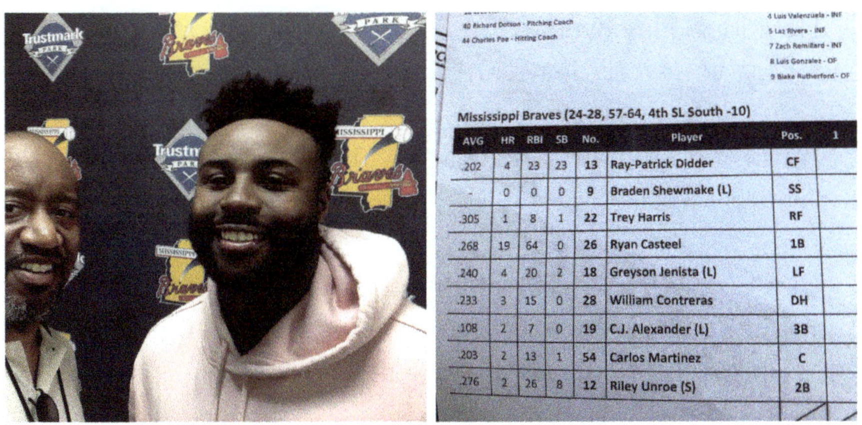

40 Richard Dotson - Pitching Coach
44 Charles Poe - Hitting Coach

4 Luis Valenzuela - INF
5 Laz Rivera - INF
7 Zach Remillard - INF
8 Luis Gonzalez - OF
9 Blake Rutherford - OF

Mississippi Braves (24-28, 57-64, 4th SL South -10)

AVG	HR	RBI	SB	No.	Player	Pos.	1
.202	4	23	23	13	Ray-Patrick Didder	CF	
-	0	0	0	9	Braden Shewmake (L)	SS	
.305	1	8	1	22	Trey Harris	RF	
.268	19	64	0	26	Ryan Casteel	1B	
.240	4	20	2	18	Greyson Jenista (L)	LF	
.233	3	15	0	28	William Contreras	DH	
.108	2	7	0	19	C.J. Alexander (L)	3B	
.203	2	13	1	54	Carlos Martinez	C	
.276	2	26	8	12	Riley Unroe (S)	2B	

Trey Harris of the Mississippi Braves gets ready after our pre-game interview. The 32nd round pick in the 2018 draft is making fast moves through the Atlanta minor league system.
Andrew Snorton

the left field seats, giving the Braves a 2-0 lead and ending Battenfield's night (6 innings pitched, allowing 2 runs on 4 hits).

From there, pitching continues to take center stage, as both teams combine for 8 hits. Kingham eventually gets the win, going 7 innings, allowing 3 hits and striking out 8 batters in the 2-0 win. The Braves' bullpen (2 innings pitched, allowing 1 hit) closes the door to preserve the win.

After the game, I experience some personal baseball "firsts", as there's literally a stat for everything; I'm actually the first person to interview Shewmake on the AA level (his debut). His youthful exuberance admits a little nervousness, but once the first pitch arrives, he just blends in with the game.

"Once that first ground ball it hit to me (as well as my first at-bat), it's still the same game. It's a great group of guys in the clubhouse, so it makes it easy to play". In building rapport with his teammates on his debut, along with his overall play, is indicative of his ascension in the Braves' system.

He adds, "Play every game like it's your last one. If you play that way, you won't leave anything to be desired".

And then I get a chance to see my old friend, the player of the game, Mr. Harris.

"It's been so long", I exclaimed to him as we both laughed and smiled. Never have I interviewed a player pre-game and he ends up being the player of the game.

And yes, his uniform has his trademark "dirty" appeal to it on top of delivering the game-winning hit. In going 2 for 3 with the 2-run homer, he explains, "The last at-bat, I focused on seeing the ball deep".

In-game action, as Braden Shewmake makes his AA debut (1st at-bat). One of the Braves' 2019 1st round picks, he is the first of any of his draft class to make AA).

Andrew Snorton

Shewmake during our post-game interview.

Andrew Snorton

It means making sure to get as solid a read on the pitch as possible before committing; clearly, the process pays off. With a regular season batting average over .300, he's clearly doing an effective job of achieving larger excellence at the plate with his smaller "sample size" (just go 3 for 10) approach.

Another game, another win. And that is ***nothing minor.***

CJ Alexander at bat for the Mississippi Braves.
Andrew Snorton

Trey Harris locked in.
Andrew Snorton

A few familiar faces as the Birmingham Barrons (a team we've covered) are in town. Nick Madigral (upper left), Ti'Quan Forbes (lower left), and Gavin Sheets (lower right) in action.
Andrew Snorton

Bright lights.
Andrew Snorton

Play hard. Get dirty. Win the game. It's Trey's (and the Braves") day.
Andrew Snorton

Afterward

Embrace something Historic

History in the making.

A few people are familiar with the term and have used it to capture the importance of different events. Clearly, sports is one of those things, including the games chronicled in my 2019 summer travels. As impressive as the games are along with the players behind them, there are two other things I experienced during the summer that are noteworthy and share history in a myriad of ways.

One captures history from an era gone by, and the other "quietly" looks at way the game shows its potential to be even better.

As for that era gone by, the next time your travels bring you to ***Birmingham, AL,*** it is imperative to patronize the ***Negro Southern League Museum.*** Located within a short walk behind the left-field walls of Regions Field, this experience is open most days of the week (with the exception of Sundays, Mondays, and major holidays), and for groups of 9 or less people, admission is free (for 10 or more people, it's $1 per person).

It's an accessible way to learn about more about players known and unknown whose professional journey started in the leagues which are the only avenues for African-Americans to play the game. While many are aware of Jackie Robinson's ascent from the league to breaking the barrier in Major League Baseball, others in-

A map of the teams, one of the incredible discoveries at the Negro Southern League Museum (Birmingham, AL).
Andrew Snorton

cluding Larry Doby, Satchiel Paige, and one of the all-time greats, Willie Mays, get started here.

And there's more.

With a wide range of panel discussions, theme days, events, and educational resources, visitors can enjoy a great way to learn about the greats of the game. It takes a meaningful look at the city and league's role within and beyond the game.

The displays of players from the area who either played in the Negro Leagues or Major League Baseball are there, including Jerry Hairston and his son, Jerry Hairston, Jr, Bo Jackson, Hall of Famer Frank Thomas, James Baldwin, along with displays for MLB Hall of Famer Reggie Jackson and a certain NBA Hall of Fame player by the name of Michael Jordan.

The Walls of Balls (including one autographed by the late Lyman Bostock) is one of a number of impressive sights at the museum.
Andrew Snorton

An impressive sign is in the form of more than 1600 baseballs authenticated and signed by players in the league through the Wall of Balls. In taking a closer look, I see one signed by a name I have not heard since elementary school, Lyman Bostock.

And it takes me back to a sad day in baseball.

The Birmingham native and son of a former Negro Leagues player (his father, Lyman, Sr, played with the Birmingham Black Barons and Chicago American Giants) has a 4 year career (from 1975 through 1978) with the Minnesota Twins and California Angels, and he complies a .311 career batting average with 250 runs batted in (averaging 75 RBI's a season). Many, including his former manager, Gene Mauch, feel he is on the brink of superstardom. Teaming up with Rod Carew (who is in the Major League Baseball Hall of Fame), the tandem develops into one of the more feared in the American League. As a free agent, he leaves the Twins for the Angels, and by September of his 4th season (1978), he is batting .296 with 71 RBI's.

But he never finishes the season.

On September 23, 1978, after playing against the Chicago White Sox, he takes time to visit his uncle in Gary, Indiana (where he lives after moving from Birmingham). While visiting with family friends, Leonard Smith, the estranged husband of Barbara Smith (one of the people they visit), pulls up to their vehicle and exchanges words with one of the people in the car. At a red light at the intersection of Jackson and 5th Street, he fires a shotgun into the backseat of the car, striking Bostock in the back of head. Three hours later (at 1:30am the next day), he is pronounced dead.

If not for this gem within a 2- minute walk of the ballpark, these and other stories, let alone their impact, would be unheard of. Taking time to read, see, and hear can take you where you have not gone before yet need to.

And the same can be told about living history.

My second visit to Coolray Field leads me to the press box and meeting Cris Jones. A fellow Bloomington, IL native, the Denver resident is a former Major League Baseball umpire (an 11-year career). Since 2005, he serves his current role as an umpire supervisor. With a focus on key areas including game coverage, observation, and instruction, he is grooming the next generation of umpires, one of the essential parts of the game.

"To see someone from the cradle to the commencement (is exciting for me); as part of their development, we take time down

A captivating view.
Andrew Snorton

to the Arizona Fall League and keep a tab on their development or lack thereof (if they should continue or look at Plan B)", he advises.

Where his journey required him to save up for 2 years to attend umpire school and training, today's students have scholarship

Archival views of the grand old game.
Andrew Snorton

Hall of Famers Willie Mays and Satchel Paige. And somehow, I got in the picture; get the picture?
Andrew Snorton

opportunities available. And with continued efforts to reach out to emerging audiences and demographics, there's improved possibilities for this challenging (admittedly, umpires need a thick skin given the dynamics of the game) yet potentially rewarding field.

While there's small turnover at the highest level (MLB), there are long-term opportunities to be a part of the game.

Jones adds, "Our average career span (for the Major Leagues) ***is 27 years;*** when the turnover is slim, it's tough (for new umpires to advance from the minor leagues to MLB), but we keep them in the system (as a call-up, akin to how minor league players get a call up to the big leagues). Chad Woodson (is one of the 2019 call-ups) who got hired in July as a Major League Baseball umpire (after a 15- year career in the minor leagues).

One preserves and shares the history of the game from a different yet necessary vantage point. The other builds a living history to enhance the game. Both are impressive and necessary stories beyond the ones shared in the photos, the interviews, and game coverage. And this is what makes minor league baseball the hidden gem it is.

While there are aspects which fall beyond the scope of this work, I do hope you are able to get a working idea what makes this game truly special. I hope you feel a part of the journey from Gwinnett, Chattanooga, Greenville, Greensboro, Birmingham, and Mississippi (Pearl), the game and individual narratives shared, the current and living history, all focused on making it an accessible, engaging, encouraging, and empowering journey.

Remember the stories, and remember the author (I know, shameless plug).

And that is ***nothing minor.***

A great talk about the game. Thank you Mr Jones.
EmoryRose Photography

Acknowledgements

I start off by acknowledging God for blessing all of us with a wide range of gifts and talents, along with the charge on all to use our gifts to the greater good and being good stewards to all. I thank my Dad for the countless times we would sit, watch, and analyze baseball games from the time I'm in elementary school through today, as well as being one of my first coaches when I played the game as a youngster. I thank my Mom for driving me to practices and games as a kid, including the epic time we spoke for about 3 hours after getting home from school, only to be late arriving for a game that's scheduled (we won that game by the way)!

My sister, brother-in-law (a big Phillies fan), and my nieces for being supportive and enjoying the game. And yes, both nieces are solid softball players.

Many thanks to my baseball coaches from Randolph to Ocean (NJ), especially Mr. Waering, Mr. Bertch, Mr Donnelly, Bud Messner, Mr. Deener, and Mr Zimmerman.

I want to thank the awesome staff and communications departments from the Gwinnett Stripers, Chattanooga Lookouts, Greenville Drive, Greensboro Grasshoppers, Birmingham Barons, and Mississippi Braves. Likewise, the fellow beat writers and commentators who cover teams in their respective areas, I appreciate some great "back-and-forth" regarding the game, especially on this level. A thank you to the Status Network for their encouragement and support in taking on this and other sports coverage.

Thank you to ***EmoryRose Photography*** (the best in Gwinnett County, GA, in 2018-19 for their outstanding photography). Even though I did most of the photography, they are a big help in covering the games in Chattanooga and Gwinnett (the second game). Continue the amazing work you do with your sports coverage and beyond.

A special thank you to the players I interviewed; taking time away from your pre and post-game routine is not easy, as players truly are creatures of habit as well as being highly dedicated to their craft. To Travis Demeritte, Adam Duvall, Travis Trammell, Tyler Stephenson, Brandon Howlett, Tristian Casas, Ti'Quan Forbes, Damek Tomscha, Touki Toussaint, Andrés Blanco, Trey Harris, and Braden Shewmake, I wish you tremendous success (but not too much if you play against my favorite team, the New York Yankees). And to think Trey enjoyed our pre-game interview so much that we had to do it again post-game (then again, he was the player of the game)!

Thank you to Cris Jones whose insight on the presence of umpiring is beyond amazing. It's definitely something worth revisiting and seeing how personnel on that level go further. I thank the grounds-crew, team coaching staffs, and all personnel who put in a tireless effort in front of and behind the scenes on game days and beyond; your knowledge and passion for the game truly comes through.

Thank you to the Negro Southern League Museum. Keep doing the amazing and needed work in preserving our history. ***It must be supported!***

To my D9 crew, especially my fraternity brothers of Alpha Phi Alpha Fraternity, Inc, don't sleep on this game. There are opportunities on and off the field for our present and future to pursue.

A special thank you goes out to those in attendance at my high school class reunion in September 2019; you truly never know who is paying attention to what you do, as one of my classmates asked me when this book is coming out. Well, it's here, so I thank you for putting it out there in the universe. And shouts to my schools: Fernbrook Elementary, Ocean Township Middle and High School, Wake Forest University, UGA, and our HBCU's. You're all needed in more ways than one, so let's make things better for all. To the bookstores, book festivals, book clubs, special events, host venues, media outlets, and of course, readers and listeners (of the audiobooks), it means a lot to have you receive and support my work. Thank you and continued blessings.

Sincerely,
Andrew Snorton (the author)

The author doing some research, as well as a cool self-photo.

Andrew Snorton

Closing Notes

Team information

Gwinnett Stripers
Coolray Field
2500 Buford Drive
Lawrenceville, GA 30043
AAA affiliate of the Atlanta Braves
Site: mlb.com/gwinnett

Chattanooga Lookouts
AT&T Field
POB 11002
Chattanooga, TN 37401
AA affiliate of the Cincinnati Reds
Site: mlb.com/Chattanooga

Greenville Drive
Fluor Field
935 South Main Street
Greenville, SC 29601
A affiliate of the Boston Red Sox
Site: mlb.com/Greenville

Greensboro Grasshoppers
First Bank National Field
408 Bellemead Street
Greensboro, NC 27401
A affiliate of the Pittsburgh Pirates
Site: mlb.com/Greensboro

Birmingham Barons
Regions Field
1401 1st Ave S
Birmingham, AL 35233
AA affiliate of the Chicago White Sox
Site: mlb.com/Birmingham

Mississippi Braves
Trustmark Park
1 Braves Blvd
Pearl, MS 39208
AA affiliate of the Atlanta Braves
Site: mlb.com/Mississippi

Contact information for the museum:

Birmingham Negro Southern League Museum
120 16th St S – Unit 200
Birmingham, AL 3233
Site: birminghamnslm.org

Site used for research on Lyman Bostock, Jr:

Sabr.org/bioproj/person/9bb77e84

Get in the game (Coolray Field)!
Andrew Snorton

About the Author

Illinois born and New Jersey raised, Andrew is based in Metro-Atlanta. His previous works ***Deeper than your deepest sleep: thoughts on love with Joseph Snorton*** (a poetic take on the action of love via multiple lenses and perspectives) and ***9 stories of faith: volume 1*** (a collection of interviews looking at how individuals work beyond their biggest daily challenges via their faith, best practices in health and wellness, support networks, and self-view), are 2019 Top-1000 reads by the Author Academy Awards. His audiobook series ***The Author's Mixtape*** audiobook series (volumes 1-3) is an organic series of spoken word and music where all work is completed in single/individual recording sessions, taking on contemporary issues for students and adults.

His work with Creative Community Solutions keeps him entrenched in the community via the education and press/media services provide. He serves as the host of The Conversation Corner television show on the Status Network, covering entertainment, business, and community news. His community activity includes his membership in Alpha Phi Alpha Fraternity, Inc (via the Xi Eta Chapter at Wake Forest University), as well as being a charter member of the Gwinnett County GA (where he served as president from 2001-04) and Loganville-Conyers, GA chapters. He is also a board member (current or former) for organizations ranging from the LEAD Foundation (Lawrenceville, GA), Family Food Festival Atlanta, and with his alma mater, including being the former president of the Association of Wake Forest University Black Alumni (2011-15), Alumni Council (2011-16), Greek Alumni Advisory Board (2017-present), Alumni-in-Admissions (since 2010), and the School of Divinity (2016-present).

Its the author. Andrew Snorton
Andrew Snorton

Author Andrew Snorton
Facebook: Author Andrew Snorton
Instagram/Twitter: @authorasnorton
YouTube: Author ASnorton
Email: authorasnorton@gmail.com
Site: asnortonccs.wixsite.com/authorpage

www.ingramcontent.com/pod-product-compliance
Ingram Content Group UK Ltd.
Pitfield, Milton Keynes, MK11 3LW, UK
UKHW021007290726
14059UKWH00001BA/5

9 780578 723587